From the Editors of
ESSENCE

A Salute to
MICHELLE OBAMA

ESSENCE

EDITOR-IN-CHIEF Constance C.R. White
EXECUTIVE EDITOR Vanessa K. Bush
CREATIVE DIRECTOR Greg Monfries
EDITORIAL PROJECTS DIRECTOR Patrik Henry Bass
PRODUCTION MANAGER LaToya N. Valmont

FROM THE EDITORS OF ESSENCE: A SALUTE TO MICHELLE OBAMA

EDITOR Patrik Henry Bass
DESIGN DIRECTOR Pinda D. Romain
PHOTO EDITOR Leah Rudolfo
PRODUCTION MANAGER LaToya N. Valmont
REPORTERS Bridgette Bartlett, Ylonda Gault Caviness
RESEARCH Christine M. Gordon,
Danielle Hester, Mervyn Keizer
COPY EDITORS Valerie A. David, Hope E. Wright

CONTENT CREDITS
ESSENCE acknowledges all the writers
who contributed to this book:
Dr. Maya Angelou, Michelle Obama, Marian Robinson,
Iyanla Vanzant, Constance C.R. White

SPECIAL THANKS
Tammy Berentson, Janice K. Bryant, Denolyn Carroll,
Michelle Ebanks, Amy Glickman, Carina Rosario

Time
HOME ENTERTAINMENT

PUBLISHER Jim Childs
VICE PRESIDENT, BUSINESS DEVELOPMENT & STRATEGY
Steven Sandonato
EXECUTIVE DIRECTOR, MARKETING SERVICES Carol Pittard
EXECUTIVE DIRECTOR, RETAIL & SPECIAL SALES
Tom Mifsud
EXECUTIVE PUBLISHING DIRECTOR Joy Butts
EDITORIAL DIRECTOR Stephen Koepp
DIRECTOR, BOOKAZINE DEVELOPMENT & MARKETING
Laura Adam
FINANCE DIRECTOR Glenn Buonocore
ASSOCIATE PUBLISHING DIRECTOR Megan Pearlman
ASSISTANT GENERAL COUNSEL Helen Wan
ASSISTANT DIRECTOR, SPECIAL SALES Ilene Schreider
SENIOR BOOK PRODUCTION MANAGER
Susan Chodakiewicz
DESIGN & PREPRESS MANAGER Anne-Michelle Gallero
BRAND MANAGER Roshni Patel
ASSOCIATE PREPRESS MANAGER Alex Voznesenskiy
ASSOCIATE BRAND MANAGER Isata Yansaneh

SPECIAL THANKS
Katherine Barnet, Jeremy Biloon, Rose Cirrincione,
Lauren Hall Clark, Jacqueline Fitzgerald, Christine Font,
Jenna Goldberg, Suzanne Janso, David Kahn,
Mona Li, Amy Mangus, Robert Marasco,
Kimberly Marshall, Amy Migliaccio,
Nina Mistry, Dave Rozzelle, Ricardo Santiago,
Adriana Tierno, Vanessa Wu

We welcome your comments and suggestions about
ESSENCE Books. Please write to us at:
ESSENCE Books
Attention: Book Editors
P.O. Box 11016
Des Moines IA 50336-1016

If you would like to order any of our hardcover Collector's
Edition books, please call us at 800-327-6388 (Monday
through Friday, 7 A.M.–8 P.M., or Saturday, 7 A.M.–6 P.M.
Central Standard Time).

FRONT COVER Photograph by Stewart Shining
(courtesy of Trunk Archive)

BACK COVER Photograph by Jason Reed
(courtesy of Reuters)

973.932
SAL

JULY 7, 2010, *Washington, DC*
First Lady Michelle Obama exits the
U.S. Department of the Treasury
following her twentieth agency visit.

contents

SEPTEMBER 6, 2012, *Charlotte, NC*
Mrs. Obama takes the stage at the
Democratic National Convention to introduce
her husband, President Barack Obama.

 APRIL 28, 2012, *Washington, DC*
First Lady Michelle Obama enjoys a
moment at the 2012 White House
Correspondents' Association Dinner.

introduction

Once in our lives, or once every ten years if we're lucky, we are participants in a moment that lifts us beyond our imaginations. The event fills us with joy and hope, and serves as a reminder of our goodness as human beings.

Michelle Obama's emergence center stage as First Lady of the United States was for many women such a moment. We know that living in the age of Michelle O, we are witnesses to history unfolding. And now that President Barack Obama has been elected to a second term, we will have more time to enjoy her in the spotlight.

The editors of ESSENCE lovingly put together *A Salute to Michelle Obama* with your affection for Mrs. Obama topmost in our minds. The book, which includes your comments, is divided into four sections: Substance, Style, Spirit and Speeches.

It is one of the most important publications we've created, a keepsake for you from the premier brand dedicated to modern African-American women. We are encouraged when we see Mrs. Obama and she says, "Tell everyone at ESSENCE I said hello. You're doing good work over there."

How history will judge Mrs. Obama, we don't know. However, we are clear on how we feel about her. Women and men speak of her intelligence, her beauty, her rightness as First Lady, her assets as not only a wife but also the wife of a historic president, the first Black man and one of the youngest men to hold the office.

As we've seen through the experiences of Betty Ford and Nancy Reagan, first ladies have often been cast in the same mold. But Michelle Obama, born Michelle LaVaughn Robinson in Chicago on January 17, 1964, has broken it.

We've heard from you, our ESSENCE family, about how much you admire what she has done, how she makes you proud. You love how she supports her husband. You believe she's a great mother to Sasha and Malia, and you appreciate how she represents Black women.

You salute her spirit in the face of difficulty, her beautiful style in clothes and accessories, her intelligence and her commitment to substantive issues like obesity, the military and the strength of family.

As First Lady, Mrs. Obama has unimaginable privileges, but we also know she faces extraordinary challenges. We know because we often face similar challenges ourselves.

We have dreams. Our mothers, fathers, grandparents and ancestors from even further back had dreams, too. And many of them have now been realized in Mrs. Obama.

We struggle to find positive images of ourselves and of our families. The First Lady never fails us. When society tried to pin another stereotype on her, she didn't back down. I felt she was defending us when she was portrayed by the press and Republicans as another angry Black woman.

Black women have a right to be angry; some of us are and some of us aren't. But we also have plenty to be happy and optimistic about. Mrs. Obama reflects the layered beings we truly are.

It's a mighty weight to carry, yet we never see her flinch. We never hear her complain. It's as if she knows full well the vast space she occupies. She understands what her smile, her grace, her style, her university degrees and her utter fierceness mean to us.

This book is for you, about a woman like you, a reader, who rose to the pinnacle of the world.

I remind women when they are hesitant to celebrate a "first" in their lives that there is only *one* first kiss. There will always be only *one* first African-American first lady of the United States.

How blessed we are that it is Michelle.

CONSTANCE C.R. WHITE
Editor-in-Chief

> **"** *She reminds us that it's okay for us to be smart, intelligent, beautiful women and want more for ourselves."*
> —LAUREN W., NEW YORK CITY

NO MATTER WHERE SHE TRAVELS—ACROSS THE U.S. OR TO SOUTH AFRICA AND OTHER PARTS OF THE WORLD— FIRST LADY MICHELLE OBAMA ALWAYS TREATS EVERYONE LIKE KINGS, QUEENS AND HEADS OF STATE.

SUBSTANCE

JANUARY 20, 2010, *Washington, DC*
In the Blue Room, Mrs. Obama
surprises a youngster during a
White House tour.

SAMANTHA APPLETON/THE WHITE HOUSE

9

A WOMAN OF SUBSTANCE

By Dr. Maya Angelou

When I was asked during the campaign to introduce then Senator Obama and Mrs. Obama, I called Oprah Winfrey. I knew she had socialized with them. I asked her, "What is Mrs. Obama like? What should I expect?"

Oprah said simply and without hesitation, "She's the real deal."

I am just so proud and so pleased to see her as our First Lady. She shows things to the world that are natural to African-American women. By that I mean her "homeliness"—her concern about growing foods for her family's kitchen and feeding them from the soil. Homegrown food is what southern Black women have always been about.

She is taking us back to our roots.

She has also—with President Obama—reintroduced the idea of romance into the American culture. Certainly past presidents have been married. And President John F. Kennedy and his wife, Jacqueline, were a beautiful couple. But when I saw the President and the First Lady dance after the inauguration—to Etta James's "At Last" of all songs—I literally wept.

It was so touching, so poignant. Lots of people had been under the impression that White people made love and Black people had sex. The way the President held her and led her. And the way she followed him... It brought me to tears.

Mrs. Obama has such an effortless grace. The clothes she wears and the way she wears them—so very beautifully—make us all feel good about ourselves as women. So much of what she wears is easily attainable and affordable to the secretaries, the teachers and all regular working women that when we see the way she is outfitted, she makes us all feel equal to her. And we feel that she is very much like us.

It's in those moments that we begin to see the fullness of her as a woman. She looks after her family—her children, her mother—just as Black women have traditionally blended generations. She loves her husband. She is intelligent. She is accessible. She is dignified but she is not aloof. She has a sense of humor but she is not a gadabout.

Michelle Obama represents all women. **—AS TOLD TO YLONDA GAULT CAVINESS**

> **What I admire most about First Lady Michelle Obama is how her light from within shines through victory and adversity, and is maintained at all times!"**
>
> **—TIFFANY T., TUSCALOOSA, AL**

> **"** She shows confidence in whatever she does, whether it's egg hunting on the White House lawn, planting in the garden with kids, or giving a speech."
> —PATRICIA C., CHESTERFIELD, VA

NOVEMBER 21, 2011, *Washington, DC*
Mrs. Obama pauses while working in the White House garden. This image was presented in *American Grown: The Story of the White House Kitchen Garden and Gardens Across America* (Crown).

JUNE 12, 2012, *Washington, DC*
First Lady Michelle Obama signs her book, *American Grown* (Crown), at an event.

NOVEMBER 22, 2010, *Miami*
Mrs. Obama joins students for a Let's Move! Salad Bars to Schools launch party.

SAMANTHA APPLETON/THE WHITE HOUSE

APRIL 13, 2010, *Port-au-Prince, Haiti*
First Lady Michelle Obama tours earthquake damage in the city, along with Haiti's then president, René Préval (next to Mrs. Obama), and his wife, Elisabeth Delatour Préval (third from right).

> **"** *I love Michelle Obama because she never meets a stranger.... Everyone is welcomed with open arms. That takes a huge emotional capacity and a big heart."*
> —ELEANOR B., LOS ANGELES

MAY 5, 2012, *Richmond*
First Lady Michelle Obama
introduces President Barack
Obama at a campaign rally.

"

She has always held her head high and stood by her husband no matter what was being said at the time, and always looks beautiful and stylish.
—TAUNYA C., JACKSONVILLE, AZ

OCTOBER 16, 2011, *Washington, DC*
At the MLK Memorial dedication ceremony, the President and the First Lady link arms with Vice-president Joe Biden, Dr. Jill Biden and Harry E. Johnson, Sr. (far left), president and CEO of the Martin Luther King, Jr. Memorial Project Foundation.

JANUARY 11, 2011, *Richmond*
First Lady Michelle Obama poses with Army Staff Sergeant La Keshia Whitmore (left) and Staff Sergeant Tyeir Pritchard Davis—both of whom are from Fort Lee, Virginia—at Virginia Commonwealth University.

MAY 6, 2011, *Washington, DC*
Mrs. Obama and Dr. Jill Biden meet in advance of their spending time with veterans' mothers and wives.

JUNE 21, 2011, *Houghton, South Africa*
Mrs. Obama visits former
South African President
Nelson Mandela at his home.

SAMANTHA APPLETON/THE WHITE HOUSE

"*Our First Lady is a classy example that a woman can demonstrate strength and support in a balanced manner.*
—ERICKA S., CHARLOTTE, NC"

Nelson Mandela By Himself

A good pen can also remind us of the happiest moments in our lives, bring noble ideas into our dens, our blood and our souls. It can turn tragedy into hope and victory.

THE AUTHORISED BOOK OF QUOTATIONS

“
*I salute Michelle Obama;
she resembles a woman
officer of excellence who is a
No Drama Kind of Mama.”*
—KAY N., ATLANTA

SONYA N. HEBERT/THE WHITE HOUSE

MARCH 8, 2012, *Washington, DC*
Mrs. Obama meets with
Ernestina Mills, the first lady of
Ghana, at the U.S. State Department.

> "She is the epitome of the everyday woman. She takes care of home while still giving back to the community. And she is active!"
>
> —ALICIA C., CHARLOTTE, NC

OCTOBER 11, 2011, *Washington, DC*
First Lady Michelle Obama and invited young guests attempt to break a *Guinness World Records* jumping jacks title.

JULY 15, 2011, *Washington, DC*
First Lady Michelle shows off her double Dutch skills during a taping for the Presidential Active Lifestyle Award.

FROM TOP: CHUCK KENNEDY/THE WHITE HOUSE; GERALD HERBERT/AP PHOTO.

SEPTEMBER 8, 2010, *New Orleans*
Mrs. Obama runs a 40-yard sprint during a Let's Move! event in the Crescent City.

MAY 15, 2011, *College Park, GA*
Dr. Beverly D. Tatum, president of Spelman
College, presents the First Lady with an honorary
degree from the historic women's institution.

SPELMAN COLLEGE
CHRIST
OUR WHOLE
SCHOOL FOR
1881

"She is beautiful and loyal, and if all that were not enough, she has the intellect to match! What an amazing role model for all women.
—MONICA R.,
MANNING, SC

 SEPTEMBER 11, 2012, *Washington, DC*
Right: President Barack Obama and First Lady Michelle Obama
observe a moment of silence on the eleventh anniversary of 9/11.
Above: The First Lady reflects at the Pentagon on the same day.

I admire Michelle Obama because she is educated and elegant. Most of all, I admire her lovely presence as a Black woman who loves her Black man."

—MELODY J., BLUE SPRINGS, MO

MARCH 22, 2011, *San Salvador, El Salvador*
The President and the First Lady toast during an
official dinner hosted by Salvadoran President
Mauricio Funes at the National Palace.

PETE SOUZA/THE WHITE HOUSE

35

BE FEARLESS

By Michelle Obama

I learned a long time ago that when you've had some success, it's not enough to just sit back and enjoy it. You've got to reach back and pull someone else up too.

I keep that lesson with me every day, whether it's as the First Lady, as a woman or as a mom. I tell my girls all the time that they are beautiful, that they are smart and that they should live life without fear of failing. I say these things because they are absolutely true and because I want to make sure they hear these words as often as possible. They deserve it. And I hope they believe it.

For 40 years now, ESSENCE magazine has given us that same encouragement. Each issue tells Black women that we are beautiful. We are smart. We are strong. Our opinions matter. We should be fearless.

ESSENCE is a community of support and a source of inspiration. Here we can be proud of ourselves and proud of one another. Here we see our contributions and our potential. We can take comfort in how far we've come and have confidence in where we're headed. In 40 years we've gone from the shadows of our civil rights victories to leading the way as business owners, professors, scientists, artists and entrepreneurs. With each step this magazine has shown us who we are and what we can be.

And we need to keep it up. I have met many women—some older, some younger—who do not have someone in their lives who tells them they're good enough, that they should dream big dreams, that their hard work will pay off.

This is why I started the White House leadership and mentoring initiative and have organized mentoring events around the country. I want to help young people see their potential, to be confident in using their voices, to own the power of their experiences and to recognize that they have an important role to play in the life of this country.

With the mentoring program in D.C., we've paired local high school girls with women on the White House staff, who spend time with them each month. The women listen to their concerns, provide some guidance when asked, expose the young girls to new ways of thinking, discuss their future, and, perhaps most important, demonstrate that they were once just like them.

Each young woman has her own strengths, her own worries, her own dreams. As I travel around the world and meet with young people from all types of backgrounds, I see some kids brimming with confidence and others who are afraid to raise their hand to even ask a question. I've met students who already have a shelf full of medals and trophies, and those who seem to shrink from their accomplishments to avoid attention or embarrassment. I've met kids ready to embrace their future and those who feel like they have no future at all.

We need to change this for them and for ourselves. Each of us can use the guidance of someone who's been down the road before—and who can help us see the possibilities in front of us. We need someone who can push back on the voices telling us we're not good enough, we're not ready or just plain no.

I was a girl who sometimes heard no, but I learned to disregard the naysayers and seek out the encouragement that got me to yes. I had a mother who pushed me, a father and a big brother who let me know I was beautiful, and an extended family and friends who were proud of me. This support set me on the path to be the professional, wife, mother and First Lady I am today.

When the first issue of ESSENCE came out in 1970, we had one Black woman in Congress. Now we have 14. We have had Black women serve as secretary of state, ambassador to the United Nations, and president of an Ivy League school. Last year we achieved another first as a Black woman became CEO of a Fortune 500 company. Black women have been crowned Miss America and American Idol; we've walked away with a Best Actress Oscar and a Nobel Prize for literature, and two sisters have Grand-Slammed their way through the tennis world.

We've come so far in 40 years, and yet there's still so much untapped potential within us. I can't wait to see what we'll do in the next 40. And if somewhere along the way we need a reminder of who we are or what we can be, we'll know where to turn. ESSENCE will reach out to us, pull us up, and show us that yes, we are beautiful; yes, we are smart; yes, we are fearless. We deserve it, and now we need to believe it.

This article was previously published in the September 2010 issue of ESSENCE.

NOVEMBER 10, 2009, *Oslo, Norway*
First Lady Michelle Obama signs the guest book at the prime minister's residence.

MARTE GARMANN JOHNSEN/OFFICE OF THE PRIME MINISTER OF NORWAY

"

I'm very grateful for everything she has done for our country and for women around the world." —BEYONCÉ

> "She wears clothes effortlessly at any price point, from prêt-à-porter to couture. Yet she keeps her role as mom in chief as her highest priority, always remembering where she comes from."
>
> **—LYNN WHITFIELD, ACTRESS**

MRS. OBAMA DAZZLES NOT ONLY WITH HER WARDROBE CHOICES BUT ALSO WITH HER ULTIMATE ACCESSORIES: CONFIDENCE AND INNER PEACE. THEY MAKE HER STAND OUT AS SHE STANDS UP FOR ALL AMERICANS.

STYLE

MAY 25, 2011, *London*
Mrs. Obama shines in a gown by
Ralph Lauren and a statement
necklace by Tom Binns.

 JULY 27, 2012, *London*
The First Lady wears a jacket
and skirt by J. Mendel.

A WOMAN OF STYLE

By Constance C.R. White

The moment we set eyes on Michelle Obama, the senator from Illinois' wife, we saw that she understood well the powerful language of style. She embraced fashion, and it wasn't long before fashion hugged her back.

At 5 feet 11, she could, as we say, carry off a look. But we appreciated that, like us, she also had hips and brown skin and full lips. She seemed comfortable in her clothes, and she fully owned them.

When I first saw her, I was struck by her tall, confident carriage and by her beautiful, elegant hands. It was apparent that her favorite thing to do with these long limbs was to give hugs.

Dressed in a black two-piece jersey pantsuit, she was raising money to get her husband elected as the first Black president. It wasn't an ordinary pantsuit, but a soft, flowing outfit that might be worn at home by a glamorous French star or at a nighttime pool party by your best-dressed girlfriend.

She bought the pantsuit, made by an unassuming designer named Isabel Toledo, at a little-known Chicago boutique. Toledo would later design Mrs. Obama's arresting lemon-hued inauguration ensemble.

We love and admire Michelle Obama for several reasons; among them is how well she has taken African-Americans' appreciation for fashion onto the world stage. She's brought vivacity and sex appeal to the White House and lifted the spirits of all women.

Mrs. Obama's style is accessible. It's an artful blend of modern utility and ladylike fifties references, and she easily mixes high and low, wearing a luxury Narciso Rodriguez dress one day and a dress by White House | Black Market the next.

Single-handedly, she woke up the fashion industry. When she wore a white gown by Jason Wu at the inaugural ball, suddenly Wu, who had struggled to establish a business, was in demand.

The Council of Fashion Designers of America gave her its 2009 Board of Directors Special Tribute Award in absentia.

How extraordinary that a Black woman should be the one—more than anyone else in history except rappers and Ralph Lauren—to put American style on the global map.

Sure, we had Jackie Kennedy Onassis; yet Jackie, with all her élan, defined her look via French fashion.

Early on, Mrs. Obama was criticized for not trumpeting Black designers enough. She has caught up, wearing Kai Milla, Stephen Burrows, Lafayette 148, Byron Lars and Tracy Reese.

That Reese, the daughter of a Detroit auto worker, dressed the First Lady, was an American fairy tale come to life. Mrs. Obama chose to wear a Reese design for her speech at the Democratic National Convention in September 2012. The speech was historic not only for its content but also for the striking image of our First Lady warm and resplendent in a shimmery salmon-colored dress, her bare arms glistening in the lights, her hair and makeup breathtaking. Yet—and this is part of her appeal—she was a picture every woman could aspire to. And they did, as Reese's name trended on Twitter that night and her company Web site crashed from the high-volume traffic.

Reese's company wisely rushed the dress into production to meet the growing demand.

For her 2011 ESSENCE cover, Mrs. Obama, ever in step with the times, donned a vintage fit-and-flare frock, knowing it was in style (and economically smart) to recycle clothes. And she knew how to work an accessory.

As she told *The View* cohosts when she was a guest on the program, add a brooch or another type of accent to a simple look and suddenly "you've got something going on."

Pins, in fact, have become a signature for her, along with belts worn high on her waist, kitten-heel shoes (perhaps she doesn't want to tower over Mr. Obama), vivid colors and shapely dresses that show off her well-toned figure.

In her embrace of style, the touch of personal flair, the well-done hair and the pride in appearance, we see many women we know in our communities but who aren't in the spotlight. We are happy to see Michelle is.

JUNE 3, 2010, *Washington, DC*
Mrs. Obama pairs a Sonia Rykiel belt with a floral dress.

MAY 29, 2010, *New York City*
The First Lady tops off her Talbots skirt with an
Azzedine Alaïa wide, perforated belt.

AUGUST 15, 2012, *Dubuque, IA*
First Lady Michelle Obama
wears an Asos dress.

*I like her simplicity,
smarts and realness.
Her clothes tell a lot
about her acceptance
of self."*
—KAREN G., BROOKLYN

 MARCH 21, 2011, *Rio de Janeiro, Brazil*
The First Lady, in a Marc by Marc Jacobs
dress, greets the crowd before heading to
Santiago, Chile, with the President.

JUNE 5, 2012, *Washington, DC*
Mrs. Obama wears a Boy, by
Band of Outsiders dress.

JANUARY 31, 2012, *Burbank, CA*
Mrs. Obama wears a Michael
Kors sweater, J.Crew skirt
and House of Lavande belt.

MAY 2, 2011, *Washington, DC*
Alongside Bo, Mrs. Obama
rocks a belted floral blouse
with wide-leg trousers.

MAY 19, 2012, *Washington, DC*
Michelle Obama smiles in a violet V-neck dress and floral brooch.

APRIL 12, 2012, *Jacksonville, FL*
The First Lady wears a Liz Claiborne dress and iridescent floral brooch.

MAY 6, 2011, *New York City*
Michelle Obama accentuates the lapel of her Ports 1961 dress with an Erickson Beamon brooch.

JULY 8, 2009, *Rome*
Mrs. Obama delights in a Jason Wu dress and vintage brooch from Chicago's Ikram boutique.

It was a once-in-a-lifetime experience for me to see a breathtaking, naturally beautiful Black First Lady of the United States, and she looked like she could be my sister." —CINDY C., ROCKVILLE, MD

MAY 9, 2009, *Washington, DC*
Mrs. Obama beams in a Michael
Kors dress and St•Erasmus
statement necklace.

MARCH 19, 2011, *Brasilia, Brazil*
First Lady Michelle Obama wears
Naeem Khan while visiting Palácio da
Alvorada with daughter Malia.

> "**What I most like about her is her sense of humor, which always shines through.**"
> —NGOZI O., BRONX, NY

JULY 24, 2009, *Washington, DC*
Mrs. Obama dazzles in a Jason Wu dress.

SEPTEMBER 4, 2012, *Charlotte, NC*
The First Lady, in a Tracy Reese
dress and J.Crew heels,
waves to supporters.

> "I look to the First Lady's style because she is always sure of herself. She knows who she is and what it is she wants to wear. And she wears it. In terms of personal style she carries the clothes; they never carry her. She is never overaccessorized, always just right on point."
> —MARY J. BLIGE, SINGER

OCTOBER 21, 2009, *Washington, DC*
The First Lady is all smiles wearing a Jason Wu blouse with a cardigan, wide belt and cropped pants.

APRIL 12, 2012, *Washington, DC*
Mrs. Obama, with daughters
Sasha (left) and Malia, defines casual
chic in a bold-hued color-blocked look.

 APRIL 3, 2009, *Baden, Germany*
The First Lady steps out in an
Azzedine Alaïa ensemble.

"
*She makes us
all feel as if
we are a part
of the family.*"
—MILLIE WHITE,
TAMIMENT, PA

MARCH 31, 2012, *Los Angeles*
The First Lady wows in a Wes Gordon
jacket and Helmut Lang jeans.

57

JANUARY 20, 2009, *Washington, DC*
The First Lady shines in an
Isabel Toledo ensemble, Jimmy
Choo heels and J.Crew gloves.

JANUARY 20, 2009, *Washington, DC*
At the inaugural ball, the First Lady
stuns in her Jason Wu dress.

MAY 24, 2011, *London*
President Barack Obama and First Lady Michelle
Obama, in a gown by Tom Ford, are flanked by
Queen Elizabeth II and Prince Philip.

 SEPTEMBER 22, 2012, *Washington, DC*
In a Michael Kors gown,
Mrs. Obama bares her
iconic toned arms.

She's the quintessential woman—she captivates the world with her heroic qualities."
—SAPPHIRA M.,
CAMBRIA HEIGHTS, NY

"

Michelle Obama has crossed all race and age lines to create an image that says any woman can stand on her own two feet with dignity, style and grace."

—SAANA M., BROOKLYN

SEPTEMBER 24, 2011, *Washington, DC*
The First Lady sparkles in a skirt by Michael Kors accented by a Peter Soronen belt.

NICHOLAS KAMM/GETTY IMAGES

NOVEMBER 23, 2009, *Washington, DC*
The First Lady, in a gown by Naeem Khan, and
the President welcome India's prime minister,
Dr. Manmohan Singh, and his wife, Gursharan Kaur.

65

JANUARY 19, 2011, *Washington, DC*
First Lady Michelle Obama, in an
Alexander McQueen gown, stands with
President Barack Obama.

JANUARY 14, 2012, *Washington, DC*
The First Lady looks striking, wearing a dress by J. Mendel.

NOVEMBER 4, 2008, *Chicago*
Mrs. Obama, in a shift dress by
Narciso Rodriguez, joins the
President-elect and their daughters.

" *She's the ultimate example of what an African-American woman can be. Her spirit is truly glowing."*
—JEAN S., MINNEAPOLIS

WHEN SHE SMILES, WE KNOW IT COMES FROM DEEP INSIDE. IT'S A PLACE OF FEELING WHOLE AND AT HOME WITH HER FAMILY AND THE WORLD, IN WHICH STRANGERS WHO MEET HER BECOME LIKE FAMILY.

SPIRIT

JUNE 14, 2011, *Berkeley, CA*
The First Lady takes a moment to
collect her thoughts before being
introduced at a local event.

 OCTOBER 3, 2012, *Reno, NV*
The First Lady beams as she talks to a
group of grassroots supporters at the
University of Nevada.

A WOMAN OF SPIRIT
By Iyanla Vanzant

As a little girl, I used to travel with my paternal grandmother, who was part Cherokee Indian and part American Black, to houses in New York's Yonkers and White Plains—where she worked as a domestic. I watched her as she'd get on her knees, scrubbing floors in these stately homes. And at some point, the lady of the house would appear—dressed in a sheath dress and fancy pearls. My grandmother would always tell her how pretty she looked.

When I look at Michelle Obama—a woman of her caliber, grace, elegance and beauty—I am reminded of my grandmother. Because seeing Michelle Obama as First Lady of the United States of America proves to me that my grandmother did not scrub those floors in vain.

When my daughters were little, I used to bake them a cake every Sunday. They knew that they were going to get a treat each week, and their eyes would light up just thinking about the sweetness. I would change the color of the frosting for them to make it extra special in their favorite colors. It might be orange, or I might make it green.

I see that brightness in Michelle Obama's eyes when I see her with her children—and all children.

She is everything I always wanted to be.

I grew up in the 1950's, when being a little chocolate girl was not fashionable. A time when a woman's voice was not allowed to be heard. A time when the wealthy and well-to-do were my enemies.

I am so very proud of all that Michelle Obama represents in her chocolate being. I am so proud of her clear voice. I am so very proud of her stance of power. Seeing her standing in front of the world as First Lady of the United States reminds me that my being is enough.

When she walks into a room with her grace, her intelligence and her beauty—stuff starts to happen.... She has that much stature, and her power will transcend and it will endure far past her terms as First Lady.

I'm proud, as a woman told she could not speak her mind, to see a sister woman of her essence serve as a model of what it means to be a powerful woman.

I've lived through many first ladies.... People say she is the Black Jackie O; I say no, Jackie O is the White Michelle Obama!

Michelle Obama is pure feminine power. There is not a trace of masculinity anywhere—not even in those powerful arms, those chiseled symbols of her strength and discipline.... We see the softness of her beauty as she uses them to embrace Sasha and Malia. It's clear to the world that her children mean everything to her, that the role of mother is a blessing, a privilege, an important responsibility. That the values she instills in them—the way she teaches them to take care of their health—these things are no less important than what a woman might accomplish in corporate America.

They don't compete with each other—these roles. She is a model to women and young girls, not just her own. We see her stand as an independent spokesperson for the things she believes in.

The First Lady has redefined what it means to be a woman of power. It's not about imitating men. She shows us that nurturing is powerful. Softness and sensitivity are powerful. Loving a man—her husband—is power. None of these things diminish her intellect, her ambition, her accomplishments; they only enhance it.

She is the very embodiment of power, and she is ours. The very presence of Michelle Obama is what our mothers and grandmothers and their mothers picked cotton and scrubbed floors for. **—AS TOLD TO YLONDA GAULT CAVINESS**

NOVEMBER 6, 2010, *Mumbai, India*
First Lady Michelle Obama plays hop-
scotch during the Make A Difference
program at the University of Mumbai.

"

She's the definition of motherhood and of a great, committed partner. A woman who stands on her own—intelligent, confident, nurturing. She encapsulates all of that, and the beauty is all of that lives in the body of an African-American woman. So, for me, she's the physical manifestation of all of the greatest attributes that make up a woman in 2012."

—VIOLA DAVIS, ACTRESS

JULY 29, 2012, *London*
The First Lady takes in an Olympic basketball game.

JULY 29, 2012, *London*
Mrs. Obama gives a hug to NBA star LeBron James.

JULY 29, 2012, *London*
The First Lady chats with NBA star Kobe Bryant.

AUGUST 13, 2012, *Burbank, CA*
First Lady Michelle Obama gives a high five to gymnast Gabby Douglas, a 2012 Olympic gold medalist, on *The Tonight Show With Jay Leno*.

"What I admire most about Michelle Obama is that she understands her power as a leader and mentor. She shows her true self and lives a life young women like us can look up to and be inspired to replicate in our own way."
—TIA C., WASHINGTON, DC

JUNE 22, 2011, *Soweto, South Africa*
First Lady Michelle Obama dances
with children at the Nanga
Vhutshilo Community Center.

> *Her presence is calming, and she makes everything look easy. Her buoyancy in spite of her critics, her support for POTUS and what she believes in, her MIC (mommy in chief) role—she is awesome!"*
>
> **—PATRICIA C., CHESTERFIELD, VA**

JUNE 21, 2011, *Johannesburg, South Africa*
Mrs. Obama leads young girls at the Emthonjeni Community Center in a dance.

JUNE 21, 2011, *Johannesburg, South Africa*
Mrs. Obama, Malia and Sasha read *Dr. Seuss* to children at a community center.

JUNE 23, 2011, *Cape Town, South Africa*
The First Lady and Archbishop Desmond Tutu bump fists after a youth activities fund-raiser.

" *I think what I love most is her confidence. She knows who she is, her position in our world, and she plays her part. She does not try to pretend to be like any other first lady, any other politician's wife, any other mother—she is just herself."*
—TIFFANY C., COLUMBUS, OH

OCTOBER 31, 2009, *Washington, DC*
The First Lady finds her inner
Catwoman on Halloween.

JULY 16, 2012, *Washington, DC*
The First Couple attend the 2012 U.S. Men's National Team basketball game against Brazil at the Verizon Center.

JULY 16, 2012, *Washington, DC*
The Kiss Cam catches the First Couple.

JULY 16, 2012, *Washington, DC*
The First Couple see themselves on the Cam.

JULY 16, 2012, *Washington, DC*
It was the kiss seen all around the world.

FEBRUARY 24, 2009, *Washington, DC*
First Lady Michelle Obama and her mother,
Marian Robinson, were photographed at the
White House for a May 2009 ESSENCE cover story.

MY TIME IN THE WHITE HOUSE

By Marian Robinson

In September I sat with my son-in-law and my two granddaughters at the White House as we watched my daughter, Michelle, give her speech at the Democratic National Convention. She was having a real impact on everyone in that arena down in Charlotte, North Carolina—and I know she did with those of us who know her best.

Watching her that night was one of those moments from the last four years that I'll never forget. But to be honest, I can't say I was surprised to see my daughter making such an impression. From my perspective as a mom and a grandma here in the White House, I see her honesty and strength every day. I see how much she loves her girls and her husband. And I see how hard she and Barack are working to make things better for folks across the country.

Now I know this might sound crazy, but even though I've been living in the White House for the past couple of years, I've got to admit that there are a few things I still miss—like that little bitty house I lived in for decades, and many of my friends and family back in Chicago. But after Barack was elected President and Michelle asked me to move with them to Washington, I said yes because I knew I'd be worrying about them if I was back in Chicago anyway. I just hoped I could be helpful.

You see, my job here is the easiest one of all: I just get to be Grandma. We didn't have much when the kids were growing up. My husband, Fraser, worked for the city water plant, and I was a stay-at-home mom for most of their childhood. Like most families, ours went through plenty of ups and downs, but Fraser and I tried to show our kids that when you fall you have to get right back up. We'd tell them that everybody goes through trials and tribulations, and the people who succeed are the ones who say, "Okay, that's just a snag," and keep on going. I guess that's just the way my husband and I lived.

We also made sure they understood that nothing was more important than their education. When I look at Michelle and Craig—a big-time college basketball coach—I feel like maybe Fraser and I got something right. We didn't do anything special. But I see the adults our kids have become and I can't help but smile a little bit. With Michelle, I see how whatever's in front of her, she'll throw her whole heart into it. Whether she's helping kids learn how to eat healthy foods and exercise, supporting our military families or inspiring young people to pursue their dreams, Michelle will always give 110 percent. And if she hits a snag, that's when she gives 120 percent.

Barack is the same way. I often marvel that the two of them found each other in the first place because they're so similar in so many ways. They both work so hard, they're both so smart, they love each other so much, and they do whatever they can to make the world around them just a little bit better. I admire how hard Barack works. And I know that he does it because he wants to make sure that this country is still a place where you can make it if you try. He wants to make sure that a college education is affordable and attainable so that all parents can encourage their kids to reach for it, just like Fraser and I did. He wants to make sure that moms and dads can provide for their families, and folks my age can retire with dignity and security. And he wants every child to believe that they can achieve their dreams, no matter where they come from, what they look like or how much money their parents make. That's what makes him work so hard. I've seen it from him and I've heard it from him. And that's why I'll be voting for him in November, and I hope you do, too.

What amazes me the most, though, is that Barack still makes time for family dinner almost every night. He's still calling out plays from the sideline for Sasha's basketball team. He's talking the girls through their days, helping them with their homework, and laughing and joking with them every single day.

So whether it's as parents or as professionals, Michelle and Barack both truly believe the words that Michelle said in her big speech: "When you've worked hard, and done well, and walked through that doorway of opportunity, you do not slam it shut behind you. You reach back, and you give other folks the same chances that helped you succeed."

That's the way Fraser and I and so many people of our generation lived every day.

A version of this article was previously published in the November 2012 issue of ESSENCE.

A woman of this caliber deserves all the recognition, admiration and respect that she has so well earned."
—**THE LATE DR. DOROTHY HEIGHT, CIVIL RIGHTS LEADER**

OCTOBER 5, 2011, *Washington, DC*
First Lady Michelle Obama thanks
U.S. Secret Service staff members for
the work they do on behalf of the nation.

> " When I look at First Lady Michelle Obama standing comfortable, tall and unapologetic—for her intelligence, for her height, for her arms, for herself—I feel smart and tall and present as well, with no explanation necessary!" —ALFRE WOODARD, ACTRESS

FEBRUARY 1, 2012, *Burbank, CA*
First Lady Michelle Obama and talk-show host Ellen DeGeneres dance to celebrate the second anniversary of Let's Move!

MAY 29, 2012, *New York City*
The First Lady and *Good Morning America*'s Robin Roberts are joined by students from P.S. 102 and P.S. 107.

JANUARY 25, 2012, *Washington, DC*
First Lady Michelle Obama and late-night TV host Jimmy Fallon participate in a tug-of-war at the White House.

I was impressed by how centered the Obamas were before they moved into the White House. And bringing Mrs. Robinson, the queen's mother, with them helped seal all the life lessons Michelle had poured into her family."

—DR. SUZAN JOHNSON COOK, U.S. AMBASSADOR AT LARGE FOR INTERNATIONAL RELIGIOUS FREEDOM

JULY 17, 2011, *Washington, DC*
The First Family attends
Sunday service at
St. John's Episcopal Church.

Michelle Obama is the walking personification of passion, poise, and persistence."
—ANGELA BASSETT

WE HEAR MRS. OBAMA'S WORDS AND, JUST AS IMPORTANT, WE FEEL THEM. NOT ONLY BECAUSE THEY COME FROM A PLACE OF AUTHENTICITY BUT ALSO BECAUSE THEY ALWAYS RING TRUE ABOUT WHO WE ARE.

SPEECHES

NOVEMBER 5, 2012, *Des Moines, IA*
Mrs. Obama speaks during the waning days of the campaign. Her husband would go on to win another historic victory the next day.

MOM-IN-CHIEF

First Lady Michelle Obama's remarks at the Democratic National Convention on September 4, 2012, in Charlotte, North Carolina, provided a turning point for the election and a triumphant moment in American political history

Over the past few years as First Lady, I have had the extraordinary privilege of traveling all across this country.

And everywhere I've gone, and the people I've met, and the stories I've heard, I have seen the very best of the American spirit.

I have seen it in the incredible kindness and warmth that people have shown me and my family, especially our girls.

I've seen it in teachers in a near-bankrupt school district who vowed to keep teaching without pay.

I've seen it in people who become heroes at a moment's notice, diving into harm's way to save others; flying across the country to put out a fire; driving for hours to bail out a flooded town.

And I've seen it in our men and women in uniform and our proud military families. In wounded warriors who tell me they're not just going to walk again, they're going to run, and they're going to run marathons. In the young man blinded by a bomb in Afghanistan who said, simply, "I'd give my eyes 100 times again to have the chance to do what I have done and what I can still do."

Every day, the people I meet inspire me. Every day, they make me proud. Every day they remind me how blessed we are to live in the greatest nation on earth.

Serving as your First Lady is an honor and a privilege. But back when we first came together four years ago, I still had some concerns about this journey we'd begun.

While I believed deeply in my husband's vision for this country, and I was certain he would make an extraordinary President, like any mother, I was worried about what it would mean for our girls if he got that chance.

How would we keep them grounded under the glare of the national spotlight? How would they feel being uprooted from their school, their friends, and the only home they'd ever known?

See, our life before moving to Washington was filled with simple joys. Saturdays at soccer games, Sundays at Grandma's house, and a date night for Barack and me was either dinner or a movie, because as an exhausted mom, I couldn't stay awake for both.

And the truth is, I loved the life we had built for our girls, and I deeply loved the man I had built that life with. And I didn't want that to change if he became President.

I loved Barack just the way he was.

You see, even though back then, when Barack was a senator and a presidential candidate, to me, he was still the guy who picked me up for our dates in a car that was so rusted out, I could actually see the pavement going by in a hole in the passenger-side door. He was the guy whose proudest possession was a coffee table he'd found in a dumpster, and whose only pair of decent shoes was a half size too small.

But when Barack started telling me about his family—that's when I knew I had found a kindred spirit, someone whose values and upbringing were so much like mine.

You see, Barack and I were both raised by families who didn't have much in the way of money or material possessions but who had given us something far more valuable—their unconditional love, their unflinching sacrifice, and the chance to go places they had never imagined for themselves.

My father was a pump operator at the city water plant, and he was diagnosed with multiple sclerosis when my brother and I were young.

And even as a kid, I knew there were plenty of days when he was in pain, and I knew there were plenty of mornings when it was a struggle for him to simply get out of bed.

But every morning, I watched my father wake up with a smile, grab his walker, prop himself up against the bathroom sink, and slowly shave, and button his uniform.

And when he returned home after a long day's work, my brother and I would stand at the top of the stairs to our little apartment, patiently waiting to greet him, watching as he reached down to lift one leg and then the other, to slowly climb his way into our arms.

But despite these challenges, my dad hardly ever missed a day of work. He and my mom were determined to give me and my brother the kind of education they could only dream of.

And when my brother and I finally made it to college, nearly all of our tuition came from student loans and grants.

But my dad still had to pay a tiny portion of that tuition himself.

And every semester, he was determined to pay that bill right on time, even taking out loans when he fell short.

He was so proud to be sending his kids to college, and he made sure we never missed a registration deadline because his check was late.

You see, for my dad, that's what it meant to be a man.

Like so many of us, that was the measure of his success in life—being able to earn a decent living that allowed him to support his family.

And as I got to know Barack, I realized that even though he'd grown up all the way across the country, he'd been brought up just like me.

Barack was raised by a single mother who struggled to pay the bills, and by grandparents who stepped in when she needed help.

Barack's grandmother started out as a secretary at a com-

JASON REED/REUTERS

NOVEMBER 6, 2012, *Chicago*
Mrs. Obama waves to the crowd before
President Barack Obama delivers his
victory speech following his reelection.

APRIL 27, 2012, *Washington, DC*
President Barack Obama and First Lady
Michelle Obama board Marine One
to visit military families in Georgia.

LUKE SHARRETT

munity bank, and she moved quickly up the ranks. But like so many women, she hit a glass ceiling.

And for years, men no more qualified than she was—men she had actually trained—were promoted up the ladder ahead of her, earning more and more money while Barack's family continued to scrape by.

But day after day, she kept on waking up at dawn to catch the bus, arriving at work before anyone else, giving her best without complaint or regret.

And she would often tell Barack, "So long as you kids do well, Bar, that's all that really matters."

Like so many American families, our families weren't asking for much.

They didn't begrudge anyone else's success or care that others had much more than they did—in fact, they admired it.

They simply believed in that fundamental American promise that, even if you don't start out with much, if you work hard and do what you're supposed to do, then you should be able to build a decent life for yourself and an even better life for your kids and grandkids.

That's how they raised us. That's what we learned from their example.

We learned about dignity and decency—that how hard you work matters more than how much you make; that helping others means more than just getting ahead yourself.

We learned about honesty and integrity—that the truth matters; that you don't take shortcuts or play by your own set of rules; and success doesn't count unless you earn it fair and square.

We learned about gratitude and humility—that so many people had a hand in our success, from the teachers who inspired us to the janitors who kept our school clean. And we were taught to value everyone's contribution and treat everyone with respect.

Those are the values Barack and I—and so many of you—are trying to pass on to our own children.

That's who we are. And standing before you four years ago, I knew that I didn't want any of that to change if Barack became President.

Well, today, after so many struggles and triumphs and moments that have tested my husband in ways I never could have imagined, I have seen firsthand that being President doesn't change who you are—no, it reveals who you are.

You see, I've gotten to see up close and personal what being President really looks like.

And I've seen how the issues that come across a President's desk are always the hard ones—the problems where no amount of data or numbers will get you to the right answer; the judgment calls where the stakes are so high, and there is no margin for error.

And as President, you're going to get all kinds of advice from all kinds of people.

But at the end of the day, when it comes time to make that decision, as President, all you have to guide you are your values, and your vision, and the life experiences that make you who you are.

So when it comes to rebuilding our economy, Barack is thinking about folks like my dad and like his grandmother.

He's thinking about the pride that comes from a hard day's work.

That's why he signed the Lilly Ledbetter Fair Pay Act to help women get equal pay for equal work.

That's why he cut taxes for working families and small businesses and fought to get the auto industry back on its feet.

That's how he brought our economy from the brink of collapse to creating jobs again—jobs you can raise a family on, good jobs right here in the United States of America.

When it comes to the health of our families, Barack refused to listen to all those folks who told him to leave health reform for another day, another president.

He didn't care whether it was the easy thing to do politically—that's not how he was raised. He cared that it was the right thing to do.

He did it because he believes that here in America, our grandparents should be able to afford their medicine. Our kids should be able to see a doctor when they're sick. And no one in this country should ever go broke because of an accident or illness.

And he believes that women are more than capable of making our own choices about our bodies and our health care. That's what my husband stands for.

When it comes to giving our kids the education they deserve, Barack knows that, like me and like so many of you, he never could have attended college without financial aid.

And believe it or not, when we were first married, our combined monthly student loan bills were actually higher than our mortgage.

Yeah, we were so young, so in love, and so in debt.

That's why Barack has fought so hard to increase student aid and keep interest rates down, because he wants every young person to fulfill their promise and be able to attend college without a mountain of debt.

So in the end, for Barack, these issues aren't political—they're personal. Because Barack knows what it means when a family struggles.

He knows what it means to want something more for your kids and grandkids.

Barack knows the American Dream because he's lived it. And he wants everyone in this country to have that same opportunity, no matter who we are, or where we're from, or what we look like, or who we love.

And he believes that when you've worked hard, and done well, and walked through that doorway of opportunity, you do not slam it shut behind you. You reach back, and you give other folks the same chances that helped you succeed.

So when people ask me whether being in the White House has changed my husband, I can honestly say that when it comes to his character, and his convictions, and his heart, Barack Obama is still the same man I fell in love with all those years ago.

He's the same man who started his career by turning down high-paying jobs and instead working in struggling neighborhoods where a steel plant had shut down, fighting to rebuild those communities and get folks back to work. Because for Barack, success isn't about how much money you make, it's about the difference you make in people's lives.

He's the same man who, when our girls were first born, would anxiously check their cribs every few minutes to ensure they were still breathing, proudly showing them off to everyone we knew.

That's the man who sits down with me and our girls for dinner nearly every night, patiently answering their questions about issues in the news, and strategizing about middle school friendships.

That's the man I see in those quiet moments late at night, hunched over his desk, poring over the letters people have sent him.

The letter from the father struggling to pay his bills, from the woman dying of cancer whose insurance company won't cover her care, from the young person with so much promise but so few opportunities.

I see the concern in his eyes and I hear the determination in his voice as he tells me, "You won't believe what these folks are going through, Michelle. It's not right. We've got to keep working to fix this. We've got so much more to do."

I see how those stories—our collection of struggles and hopes and dreams—I see how that's what drives Barack Obama every single day.

And I didn't think it was possible, but let me tell you, today, I love my husband even more than I did four years ago, even more than I did 23 years ago, when we first met.

I love that he's never forgotten how he started. I love that we can trust Barack to do what he says he's going to do, even when it's hard—especially when it's hard.

I love that for Barack, there is no such thing as "us" and "them"—he doesn't care whether you're a Democrat, a Republican, or none of the above; he knows that we all love our country. And he is always ready to listen to good ideas. He's always looking for the very best in everyone he meets.

And I love that even in the toughest moments, when we're all sweating it—when we're worried that the bill won't pass, and it seems like all is lost—Barack never lets himself get distracted by the chatter and the noise.

Just like his grandmother, he just keeps getting up and moving forward—with patience and wisdom, and courage and grace.

And he reminds me that we are playing a long game here, and that change is hard, and change is slow, and it never happens all at once.

MARCH 11, 2011, *Washington, DC*
NHL leaders and the Chicago Blackhawks,
Stanley Cup champions, present Mrs. Obama
with a jersey during a Let's Move! event.

But eventually we get there, we always do.

We get there because of folks like my dad, folks like Barack's grandmother—men and women who said to themselves, "I may not have a chance to fulfill my dreams, but maybe my children will, maybe my grandchildren will."

See, so many of us stand here tonight because of their sacrifice, and longing, and steadfast love because time and again, they swallowed their fears and doubts and did what was hard.

So today, when the challenges we face start to seem overwhelming—or even impossible—let us never forget that doing the impossible is the history of this nation. It is who we are as Americans. It is how this country was built.

And if our parents and grandparents could toil and struggle for us—if they could raise beams of steel to the sky, send a man to the moon, connect the world with the touch of a button—then surely we can keep on sacrificing and building for our own kids and grandkids, right?

And if so many brave men and women could wear our country's uniform and sacrifice their lives for our most fundamental rights, then surely we can do our part as citizens of this great democracy to exercise those rights. Surely we can get to the polls on Election Day and make our voices heard.

If farmers and blacksmiths could win independence from an empire, if immigrants could leave behind everything they knew for a better life on our shores, if women could be dragged to jail for seeking the vote, if a generation could defeat a depression and define greatness for all time, if a young preacher could lift us to the mountaintop with his righteous dream, and if proud Americans can be who they are and boldly stand at the altar with who they love, then surely, surely we can give everyone in this country a fair chance at that great American Dream.

Because in the end, more than anything else, that is the story of this country—the story of unwavering hope grounded in unyielding struggle.

That is what has made my story, and Barack's story, and so many other American stories possible.

And I say all of this tonight not just as First Lady, and not just as a wife.

You see, at the end of the day, my most important title is still mom-in-chief.

My daughters are still the heart of my heart and the center of my world.

But today, I have none of those worries from four years ago about whether Barack and I were doing what was best for our girls.

Because today, I know from experience that if I truly want to leave a better world for my daughters, and all our sons and daughters, if we want to give all our children a foundation for their dreams and opportunities worthy of their promise, if we want to give them that sense of limitless possibility—that belief that here in America, there is always something better out there if you're willing to work for it—then we must work like never before. And we must once again come together and stand together for the man we can trust to keep moving this great country forward—my husband, our President, Barack Obama.

Thank you, God bless you, and God bless America.

NOVEMBER 5, 2012, *Des Moines, IA*
Mrs. Obama talks to a massive crowd
before President Obama speaks at his final
rally as a candidate for the U.S. Presidency.

MAY 28, 2012, *Arlington, VA*
On Memorial Day Mrs. Obama arrives for the
wreath-laying ceremony at the Tomb of the
Unknowns in Arlington National Cemetery.

ONE NATION

Michelle Obama's speech at the Democratic National Convention in Denver, Colorado, on August 25, 2008, was eagerly anticipated. As she took the stage and shared her remarkable American journey, her words resonated around the world

As you might imagine, for Barack, running for president is nothing compared to that first game of basketball with my brother Craig.

I can't tell you how much it means to have Craig and my mom here tonight. Like Craig, I can feel my dad looking down on us, just as I've felt his presence in every grace-filled moment of my life.

With Craig at 6 foot 6, I've often felt like he was looking down on me too, literally. But the truth is, both when we were kids and today, Craig wasn't looking down on me—he was watching over me.

And he's been there for me every step of the way since that clear day in February, 19 months ago, when—with little more than our faith in each other and a hunger for change—we joined my husband, Barack Obama, on the improbable journey that has led us to this moment.

But each of us also comes here tonight by way of our own improbable journey.

I come here tonight as a sister, blessed with a brother who is my mentor, my protector, and my lifelong friend.

And I come here as a wife who loves my husband and believes he will be an extraordinary president.

And I come here as a mom whose girls are the heart of my heart and the center of my world—they're the first things I think about when I wake up in the morning, and the last thing I think about before I go to bed at night. Their future and all our children's future—is my stake in this election.

And I come here as a daughter—raised on the South Side of Chicago by a father who was a blue collar city worker and a mother who stayed at home with my brother and me. My mother's love has always been a sustaining force for our family, and one of my greatest joys is seeing her integrity, her compassion, her intelligence reflected in my daughters.

My dad was our rock. And, although he was diagnosed with multiple sclerosis in his early thirties, he was our provider, he was our champion, our hero. But as he got sicker, it got harder for him to walk; it took him longer to get dressed in the morning. But if he was in pain, he never let on. He never stopped smiling and laughing—even while struggling to button his shirt, even while using two canes to get himself across the room to give my mom a kiss. He just woke up a little earlier and worked a little harder.

He and my mom poured everything they had into me and Craig. It was the greatest gift a child could receive: never doubting for a single minute that you're loved, and cherished, and have a place in this world. And thanks to their faith and their hard work, we both were able to go on to college. So I know firsthand from their lives—and mine—that the American Dream endures.

And you know, what struck me when I first met Barack was that even though he had this funny name, even though he'd grown up all the way across the continent in Hawaii, his family was so much like mine. He was raised by grandparents who were working-class folks just like my parents, and by a single mother who struggled to pay the bills just like we did. Like my family, they scrimped and saved so that he could have opportunities that they never had for themselves. And Barack and I were raised with so many of the same values: like you work hard for what you want in life; that your word is your bond and you do what you say you're going to do; that you treat people with dignity and respect, even if you don't know them, and even if you don't agree with them.

And Barack and I set out to build lives guided by these values, and to pass them on to the next generation. Because we want our children—and all children in this nation—to know that the only limit to the height of your achievements is the reach of your dreams and your willingness to work for them.

And as our friendship grew, and I learned more about Barack, he introduced me to the work he'd done when he first moved to Chicago after college. You see, instead of going to Wall Street, Barack went to work in neighborhoods that had been devastated by the closing of steel plants. Jobs dried up. And Barack was invited back to speak to people from those neighborhoods about how to rebuild their community.

And the people gathered together that day were ordinary folks doing the best they could to build a good life. See, they were parents trying to get by from paycheck to paycheck; grandparents trying to get it together on a fixed income; men frustrated that they couldn't support their families after their jobs disappeared. Those folks weren't asking for a handout or a shortcut. They were ready to work—they wanted to contribute. They believed—like you and I believe—that America should be a place where you can make it if you try.

And Barack stood up that day and spoke words that have stayed with me ever since. He talked about "the world as it is" and "the world as it should be." And he said that all too often, we accept the distance between the two, and we settle for the world as it is—even when it doesn't reflect our values and aspirations. But he reminded us that we also know what the world should look like. He said we know what fairness and justice and opportunity look like. And he urged us to believe in ourselves—to find the strength within ourselves to strive for the world as it should be. And isn't that the great American story?

It's the story of men and women gathered in churches and

union halls and high school gyms—people who stood up and marched and risked everything they had—refusing to settle, determined to mold our future into the shape of our ideals.

It is because of their will and determination that this week we celebrate two anniversaries: the 88th anniversary of women winning the right to vote and the 45th anniversary of that hot summer day when Dr. King lifted our sights and our hearts with his dream for our nation.

I stand here today at the crosscurrents of that history—knowing that my piece of the American Dream is a blessing hard won by those who came before me. All of them driven by the same conviction that drove my dad to get up an hour early each day to painstakingly dress himself for work. The same conviction that drives the men and women I've met all across this country:

People who work the day shift, kiss their kids good night, and head out for the night shift—without disappointment, without regret—see that good night kiss as a reminder of everything they're working for.

The military families who say grace each night with an empty seat at the table. The servicemen and -women who love this country so much, they leave those they love most to defend it.

The young people across America serving our communities—teaching children, cleaning up neighborhoods, caring for the least among us each and every day.

People like Hillary Clinton, who put those 18 million cracks in that glass ceiling so that our daughters—and our sons—can dream a little bigger and aim a little higher.

People like Joe Biden, who has never forgotten where he came from and never stopped fighting for folks who work long hours and face long odds and need someone on their side again.

All of us driven by a simple belief that the world as it is just won't do—that we have an obligation to fight for the world as it should be.

And that is the thread that connects our hearts. That is the thread that runs through my journey and Barack's journey and so many other improbable journeys that have brought us here tonight, where the current of history meets this new tide of hope.

And, you see, that is why I love this country.

And in my own life, in my own small way, I've tried to give back to this country that has given me so much. That's why I left a job at a big law firm for a career in public service, working to empower young people to volunteer in their communities. Because I believe that each of us—no matter what our age or background or walk of life—each of us has something to contribute to the life of this nation.

It's a belief Barack shares—a belief at the heart of his life's work.

It's what he did all those years ago, on the streets of Chicago, setting up job training to get people back to work and after school programs to keep kids safe—working block by block to help people lift up their families.

It's what he did in the Illinois Senate, moving people from welfare to jobs, passing tax cuts for hardworking families, and making sure women get equal pay for equal work.

It's what he's done in the United States Senate, fighting to ensure that the men and women who serve this country are welcomed home not just with medals and parades, but with good jobs and benefits and health care—including mental health care.

See, that's why Barack's running—to end the war in Iraq responsibly, to build an economy that lifts every family, to make sure health care is available for every American, and to make sure every child in this nation has a world class education all the way from preschool to college. That's what Barack Obama will do as president of the United States of America.

He'll achieve these goals the same way he always has—by bringing us together and reminding us how much we share and how alike we really are. You see, Barack doesn't care where you're from, or what your background is, or what party—if any—you belong to. That's just not how he sees the world. He knows that thread that connects us—our belief in America's promise, our commitment to our children's future. He knows that that thread is strong enough to hold us together as one nation even when we disagree.

It was strong enough to bring hope to those neighborhoods in Chicago.

It was strong enough to bring hope to the mother he met who was worried about her child in Iraq; hope to the man who's unemployed and can't afford gas to find a job; hope to the student working nights to pay for her sister's health care, sleeping just a few hours a day. And it was strong enough to bring hope to people who came out on a cold Iowa night and became the first voices in this chorus for change that has been echoed by millions of Americans from every corner of this nation.

Millions of Americans who know that Barack understands their dreams; millions of Americans who know that Barack will fight for people like them, and that Barack will finally bring the change we need.

And in the end, after all that's happened these past 19 months, the Barack Obama I know today is the same man I fell in love with 19 years ago. He's the same man who drove me and our new baby daughter home from the hospital ten years ago this summer, inching along at a snail's pace, peering anxiously at us in the rearview mirror, feeling the whole weight of her future in his hands, determined to give her everything he'd struggled so hard for himself, determined to give her something he never had: the affirming embrace of a father's love.

And as I tuck that little girl and her little sister into bed at night, I think about how one day, they'll have families of their own. And how one day, they—and your sons and daughters—will tell their own children about what we did together in this election. They'll tell them how this time, we listened to our hopes, instead of our fears. How this time, we decided to stop doubting and to start dreaming. How this time, in this great country—where a girl from the South Side of Chicago can go to college and law school, and the son of a single mother from Hawaii can go all the way to the White House—that we committed ourselves, we committed ourselves to building the world as it should be.

So tonight, in honor of my father's memory and my daughters' future—out of gratitude for those whose triumphs we mark this week and those whose everyday sacrifices have brought us to this moment—let us devote ourselves to finishing their work; let us work together to fulfill their hopes; and let us stand together to elect Barack Obama president of the United States of America.

Thank you, God bless you, and God bless America.

OCTOBER 22, 2012, *Davie, FL*
Mrs. Obama addresses supporters
at Broward College. President Obama
would eventually capture the state of Florida.

TAIMY ALVAREZ/MCT/ABACA

I've known from the start that she is a Phenomenal Woman."
—DR. MAYA ANGELOU

NOVEMBER 6, 2012, *Chicago*
Mrs. Obama with President
Obama and daughters
Malia and Sasha.

Michelle
THROUGH THE YEARS

SEPTEMBER 3, 2012, *Charlotte, NC*
The "First Lady of Fabulous" was seen throughout the Democratic National Convention and around the world.

2-13